BUG BOOKS

Caterpillar

Karen Hartley, Chris Macro, and Philip Taylor

Heinemann Library
Chicago, Illinois

© 1999, 2006 Heinemann Library
a division of Reed Elsevier Inc.
Chicago, Illinois

Customer Service 888-454-2279
Visit our website at www.heinemannraintree.com

Designed by Ron Kamen, Michelle Lisseter, and Bridge Creative Services Limited
Illustrations by Alan Fraser at Pennant Illustration
Printed in China by South China Printing Company

10 09 08 07 06
10 9 8 7 6 5 4 3 2 1

New edition ISBN: 1-4034-8294-2 (hardcover)
              1-4034-8307-8 (paperback)

The Library of Congress has cataloged the first edition as follows:
Hartley, Karen, 1949-
        Caterpillar / Karen Hartley, Chris Macro, and Philip Taylor.
            p. cm. -- (Bug books)
        Includes bibliographical references and index.
        Summary: A simple introduction to the physical characteristics, diet, life cycle, predators,
                habitat, and lifespan of caterpillars.
        ISBN 1-57572-795-1 (lib. bdg.)
        1. Caterpillars—Juvenile literature. [1. Caterpillars.] I. Macro, Chris, 1940-. II. Taylor,
            Philip, 1949- III. Title. IV. Series.
        QL544.2.H385   1999
        595.78'139—dc21   98-42676
                                 CIP
                                 AC

Acknowledgments
The author and publishers are grateful to the following for permission to reproduce photographs:
Ardea: I Beames pp. 22, 27, J Mason pp. 7, 9, 17, 25, E Lindgren p. 19, A Weaving p. 18, W
Weisser p. 10; Bruce Coleman Ltd: B Glover p. 16, A Purcell p. 23, K Taylor pp. 6, 15, 20; Garden
and Wildlife Matters: pp. 4, 14, 21, 24; NHPA: Robert Thompson p. 5; Trevor Clifford: pp. 28, 29;
Oxford Scientific Films: J Cooke pp. 8, 11; Mantis Wildlife Films pp. 12, 13.

Cover photograph reproduced with permission of Getty Images/National Geographic Society.

The publishers would like to thank Nancy Harris for her assistance in the preparation of this book.

Some words are shown in bold, **like this**. You can find out what they mean
by looking in the glossary.

Contents

What Are Caterpillars?

Caterpillars are **insects**. When they grow up they have six legs. They are not caterpillars all their lives. They change into something very different.

There are many different types of caterpillars. Some turn into **butterflies**. Others turn into **moths**, like this one.

Caterpillars have six normal legs at the front. They have more legs farther down their bodies.

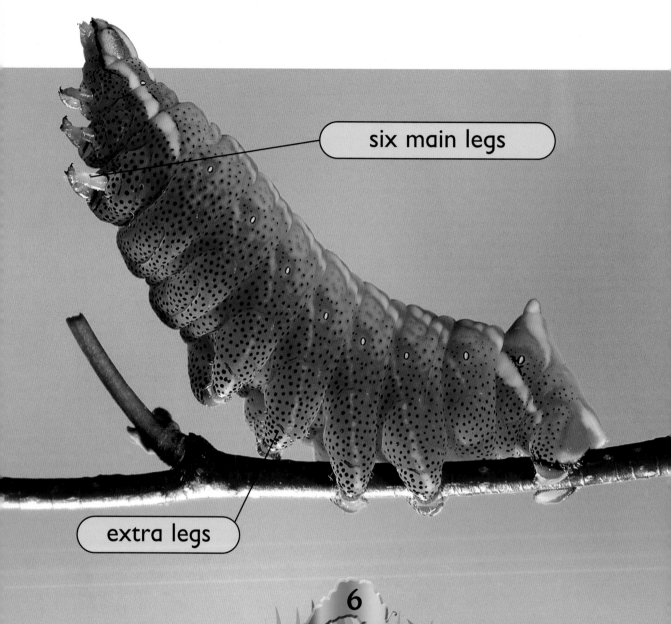

six main legs

extra legs

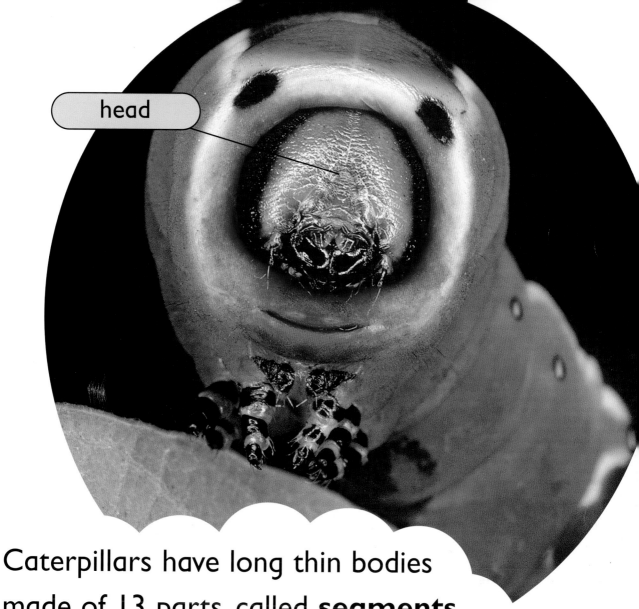

head

Caterpillars have long thin bodies
made of 13 parts, called **segments**.
The head is the segment at the front.

How Big Are Caterpillars?

Caterpillars are tiny when they **hatch** out of their eggs. They grow very quickly.

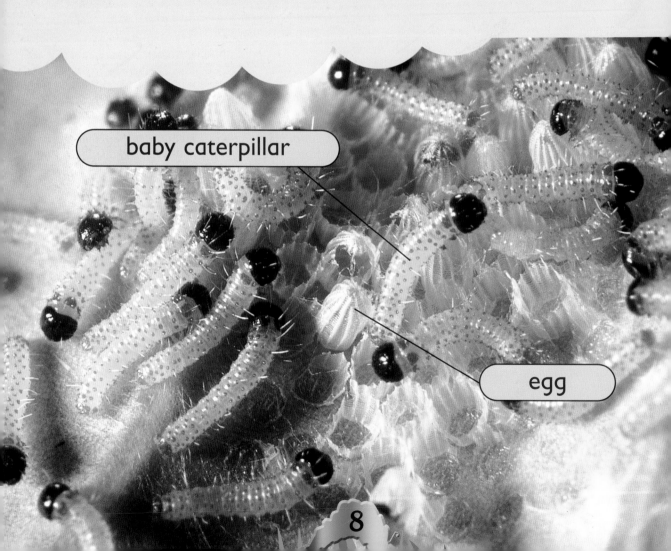

baby caterpillar

egg

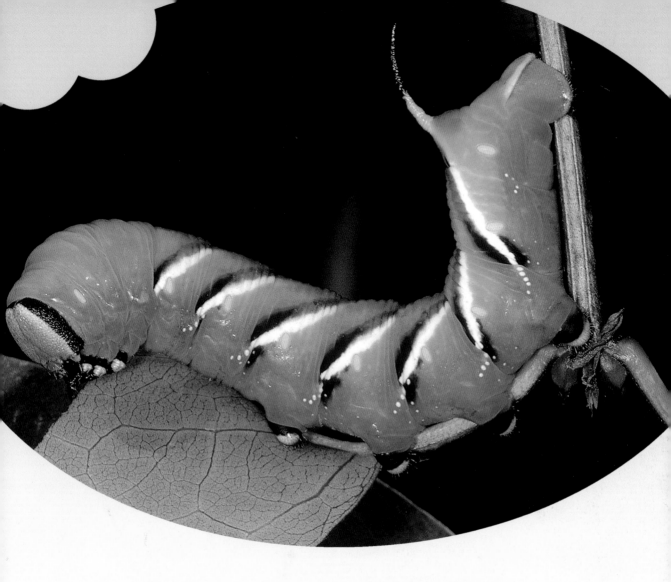

Some caterpillars grow to be as long as your little finger. Others, like the one in the picture, grow much longer.

How Are Caterpillars Born?

Female butterflies and **moths** lay tiny eggs on the leaves of plants. Caterpillars **hatch** from these eggs. They eat the leaves.

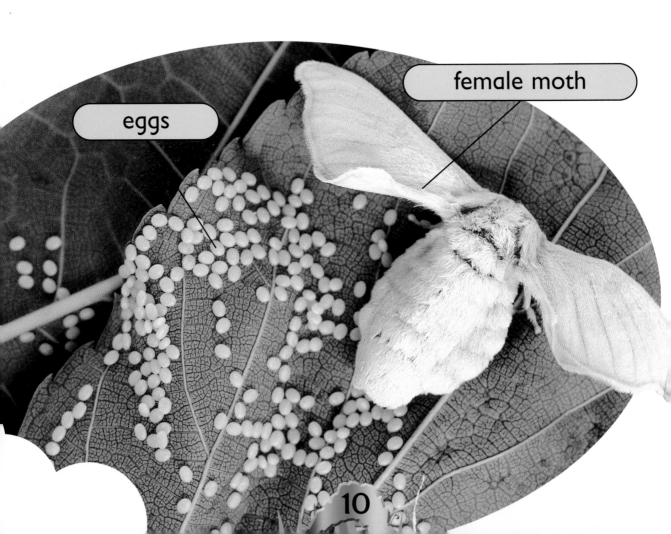

eggs

female moth

There are lots of eggs, but many caterpillars die before they are fully grown.

baby caterpillar

egg

How Do Caterpillars Grow?

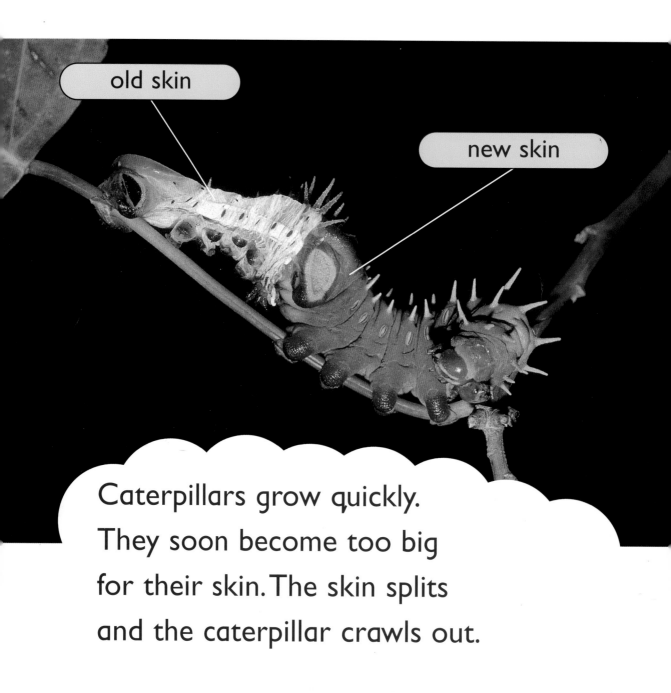

old skin

new skin

Caterpillars grow quickly.
They soon become too big
for their skin. The skin splits
and the caterpillar crawls out.

A new skin has grown underneath the old one. This is called **molting**. Caterpillars molt from their skins about five times.

What Do Caterpillars Eat?

Caterpillars eat the leaves of plants.
Many caterpillars eat grasses, vines,
and bushes.

jaws

Caterpillars have very strong **jaws** for eating quickly.

Which Animals Eat Caterpillars?

Many birds eat caterpillars. Some caterpillars are brightly colored. This tells birds that they are poisonous.

Some caterpillars have colors that make them look like sticks or leaves. This is to help them hide from birds. Other caterpillars have mean-looking faces that scare the birds away.

How Do Caterpillars Move?

Caterpillars move by using their
legs. They use their front and
back legs for different things.

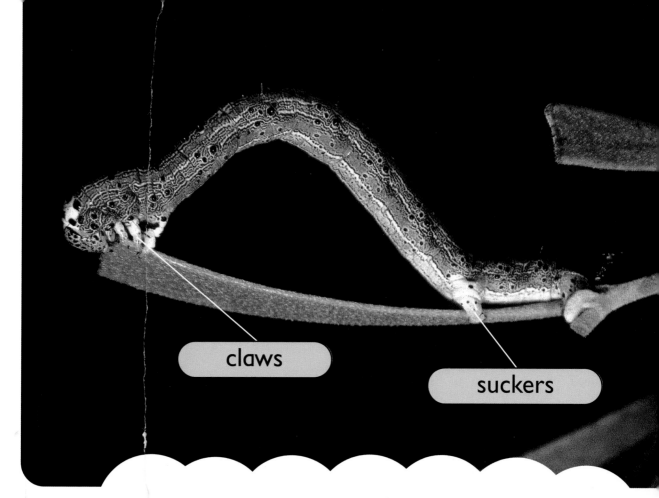

claws

suckers

The front legs have claws for holding food. The other legs have suckers for clinging to smooth surfaces. Some caterpillars make a loop with their bodies when they move.

Where Do Caterpillars Live?

Caterpillars are found
in fields, woods, parks,
and gardens.

Caterpillars live on the leaves
of the plants that they eat.

What Do Caterpillars Do?

Caterpillars spend their lives eating. They need to grow as big as they can in a short time. When they are fully grown the last skin splits.

When a caterpillar has lost its last
skin it is called a **pupa**. It is almost
ready to change into a **butterfly**
or a **moth**.

Some caterpillars spin **cocoons** around themselves before turning into a **pupa**. Some hide under the ground.

cocoon

Sometimes caterpillars **hibernate**. This means they sleep through the winter months. Some hide in cracks in trees. This keeps them safe from animals and birds.

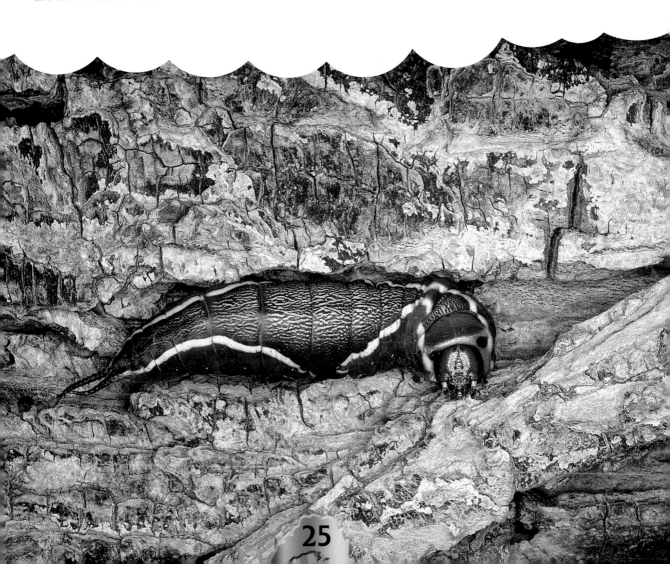

How Are Caterpillars Special?

A caterpillar has four very different stages in its short life. First it is an egg. Next it becomes a caterpillar. Then it becomes a **pupa** with a hard shell.

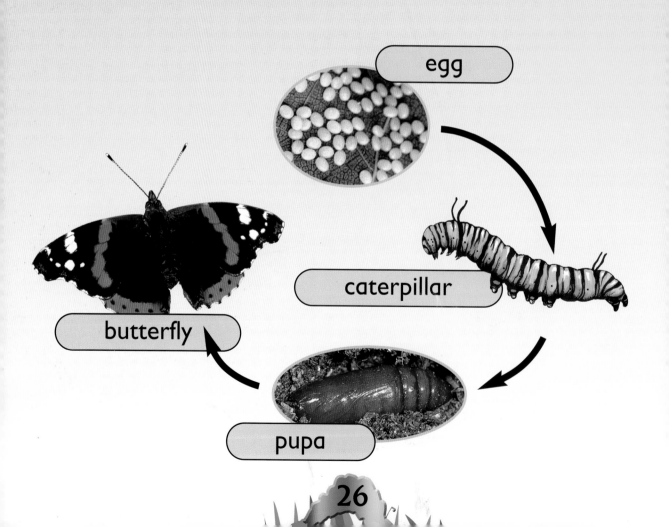

egg

caterpillar

butterfly

pupa

After about two weeks the pupa splits. This caterpillar has become a **butterfly**. It now has wings and only six legs.

Thinking About Caterpillars

This boy has found a caterpillar. It has crawled onto his hand and he is watching it. He wants to keep watching the caterpillar at home.

His friend has found an empty jar to use as a home for the caterpillar. What will they have to put in the jar so it can live there for a few days?

Keep your fingers away from hairy caterpillars, or you might be stung.

Bug Map

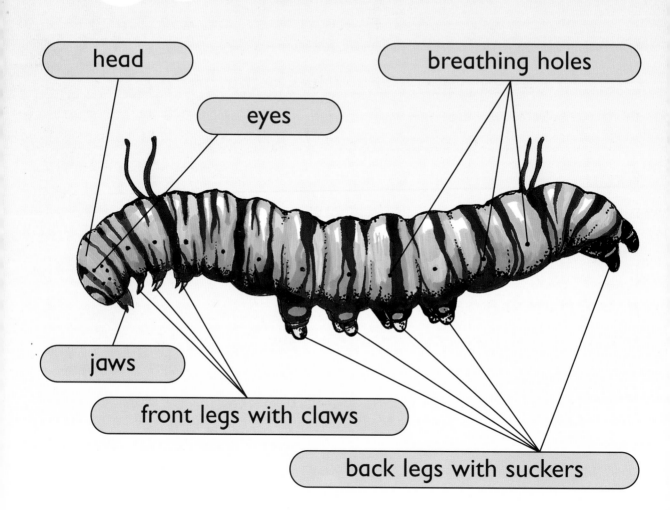

head

breathing holes

eyes

jaws

front legs with claws

back legs with suckers

Actual size

Glossary

butterfly type of insect with four large wings. Most butterflies fly during the day.

cocoon case made from a sticky thread that the caterpillar winds around itself for protection

female girl

hatch when a baby animal comes out of its egg

hibernate to sleep through the winter months

insect small animal with six legs

jaws mouth parts

moth type of insect that has large, very thin wings. Most moths fly at night.

molting when a caterpillar grows too big for its skin, it grows a new one and slides out of the old one

pupa a caterpillar becomes a pupa when it is fully grown. The pupa is very hard. The caterpillar is changing into a butterfly or moth.

segments small sections of the body that are joined together, one after another

Index

More Books to Read

Pyers, Greg. *Butterflies Up Close.* Chicago: Raintree, 2005.